Mermaids & Mandalas

Illustrated by Rex Findley

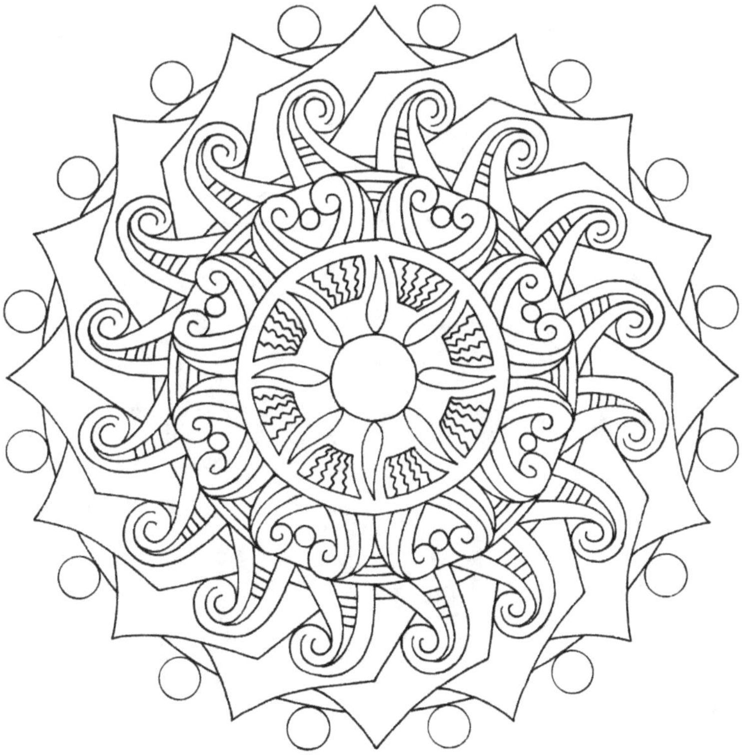

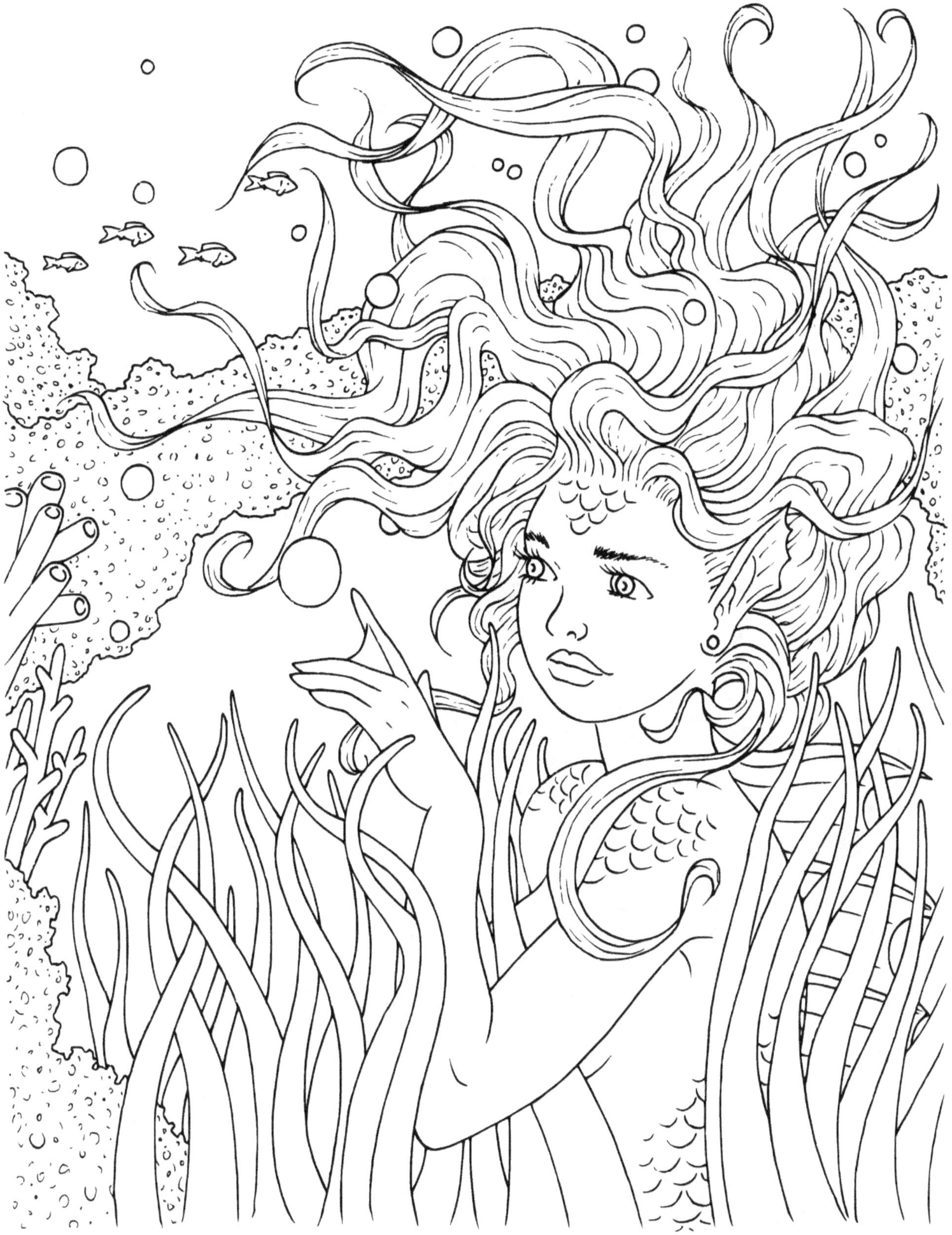

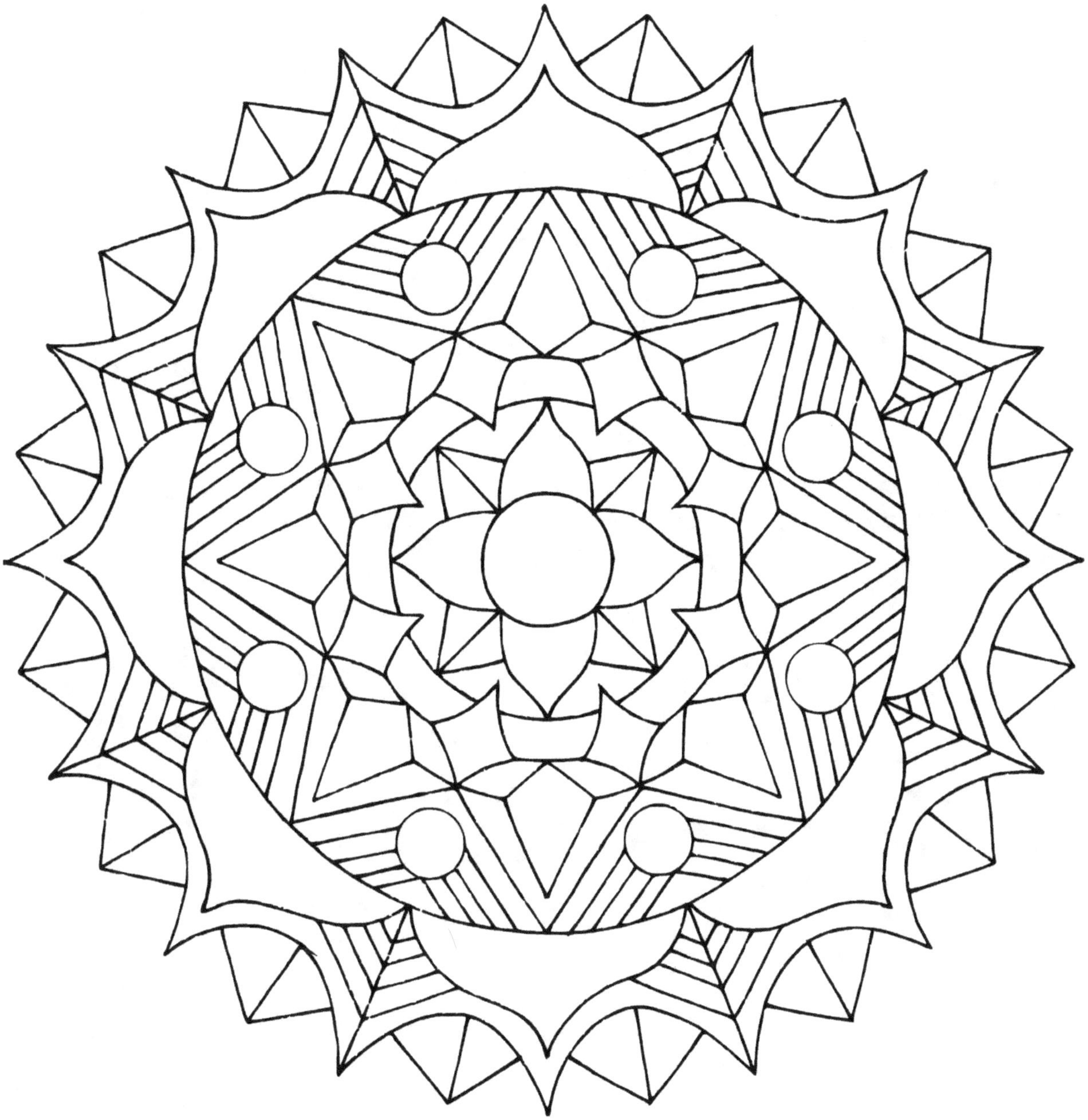

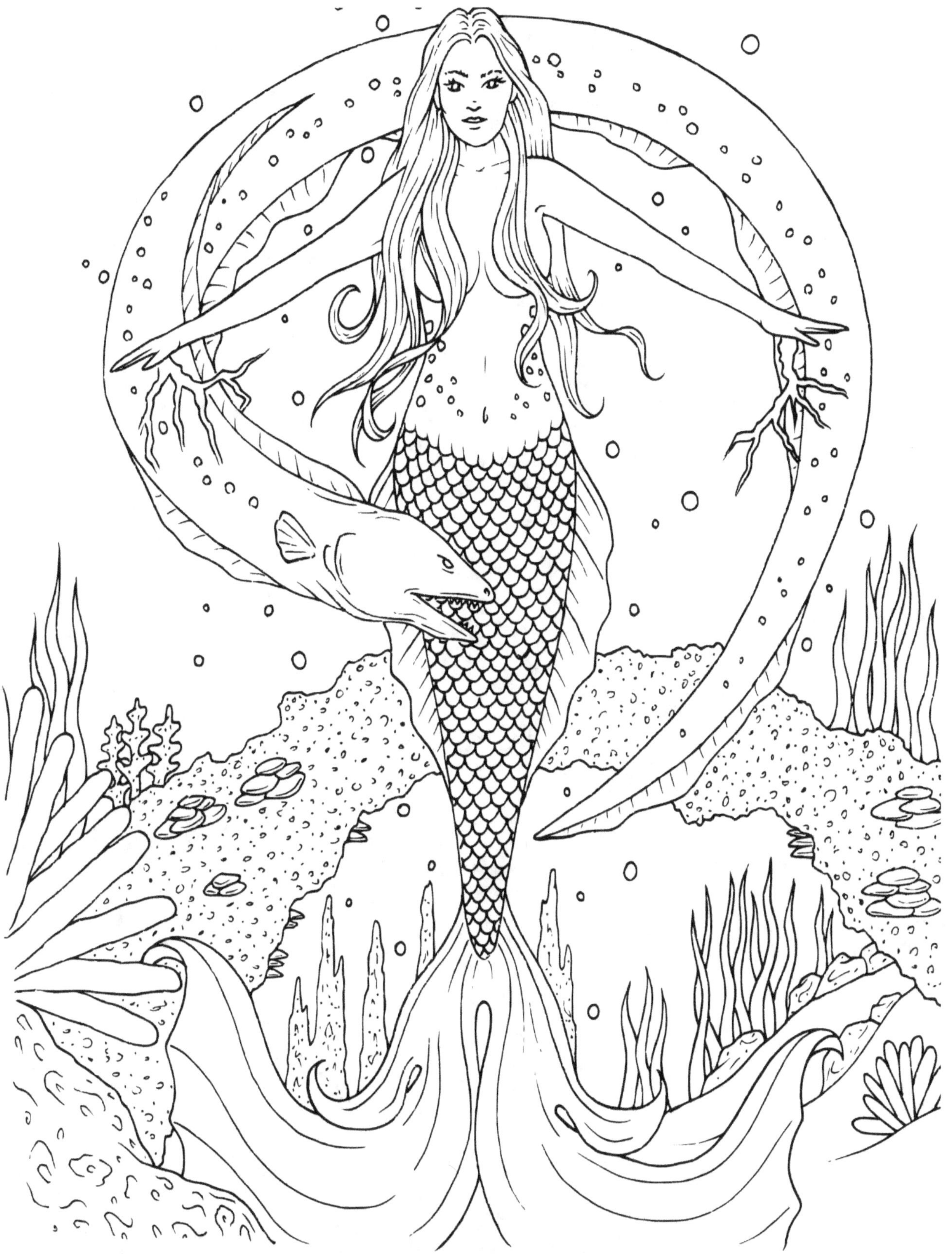

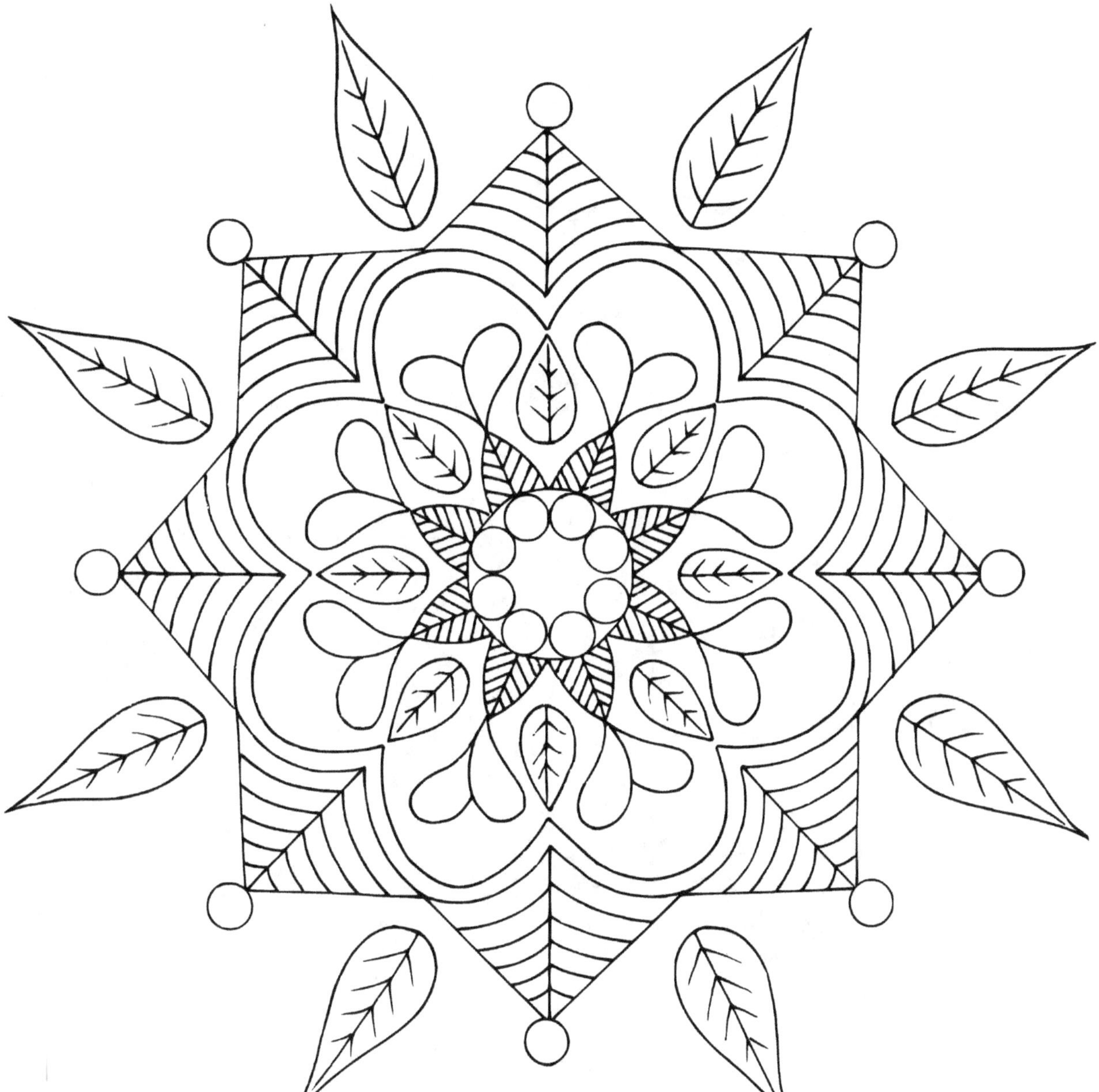

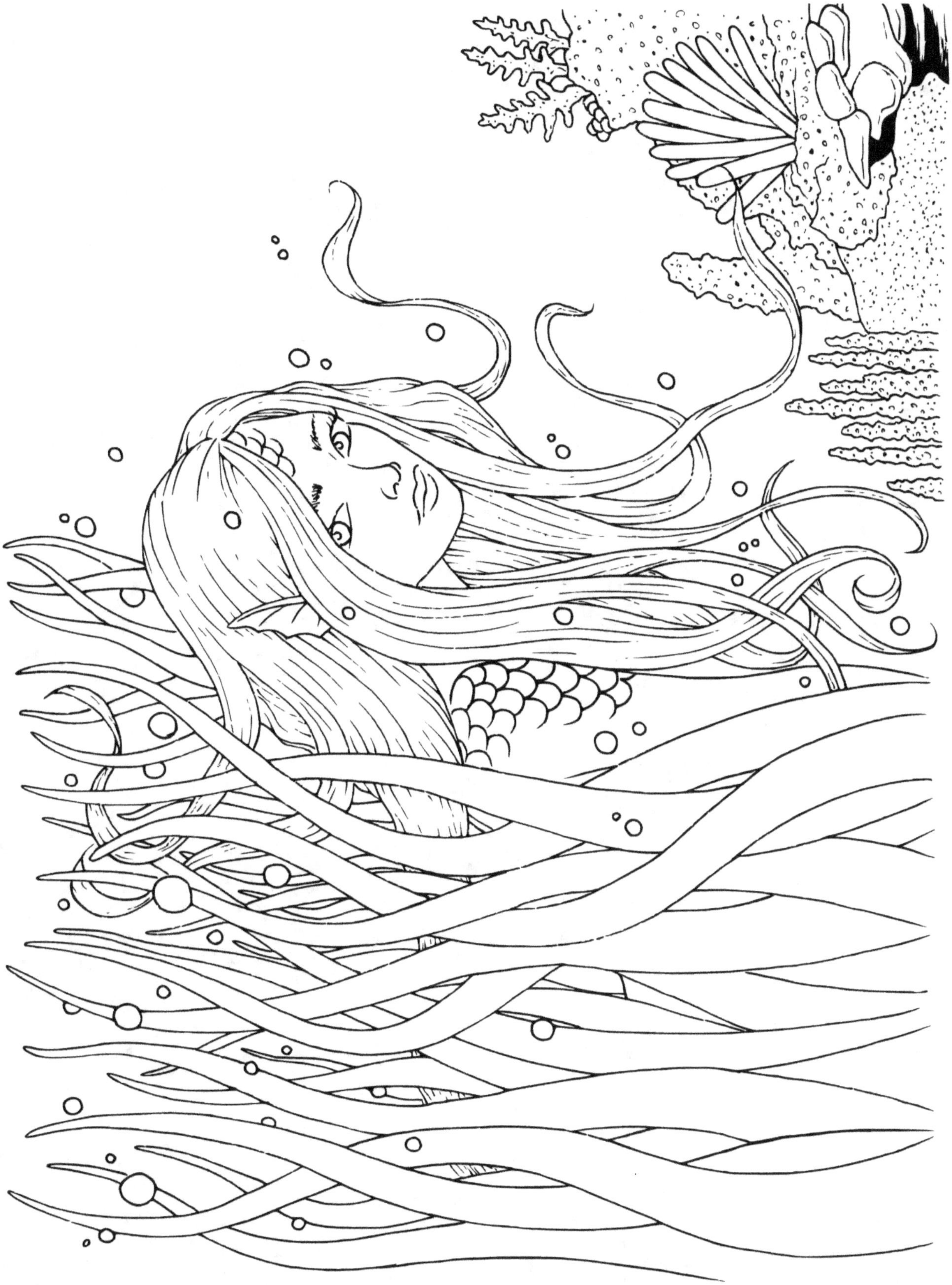

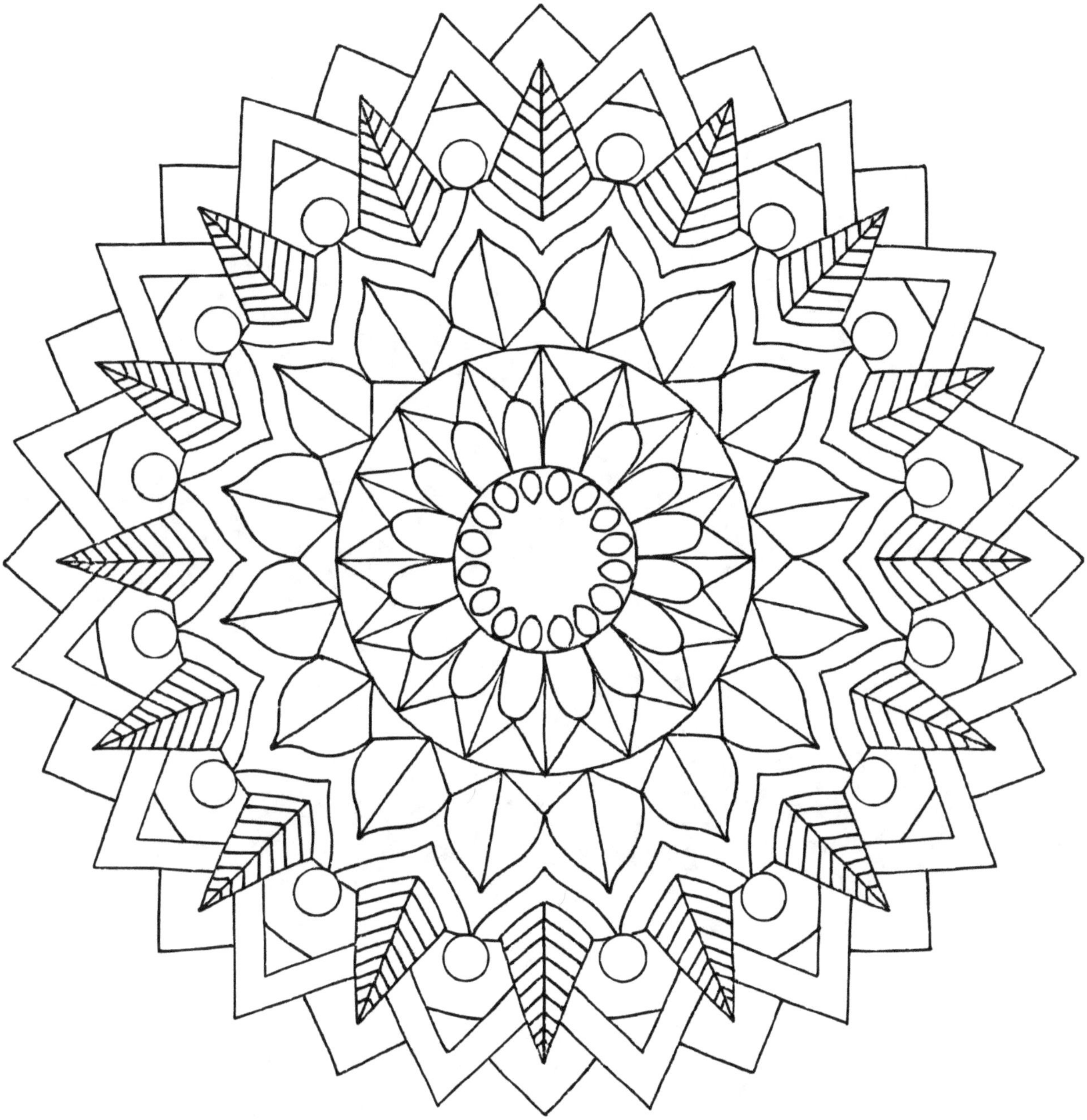

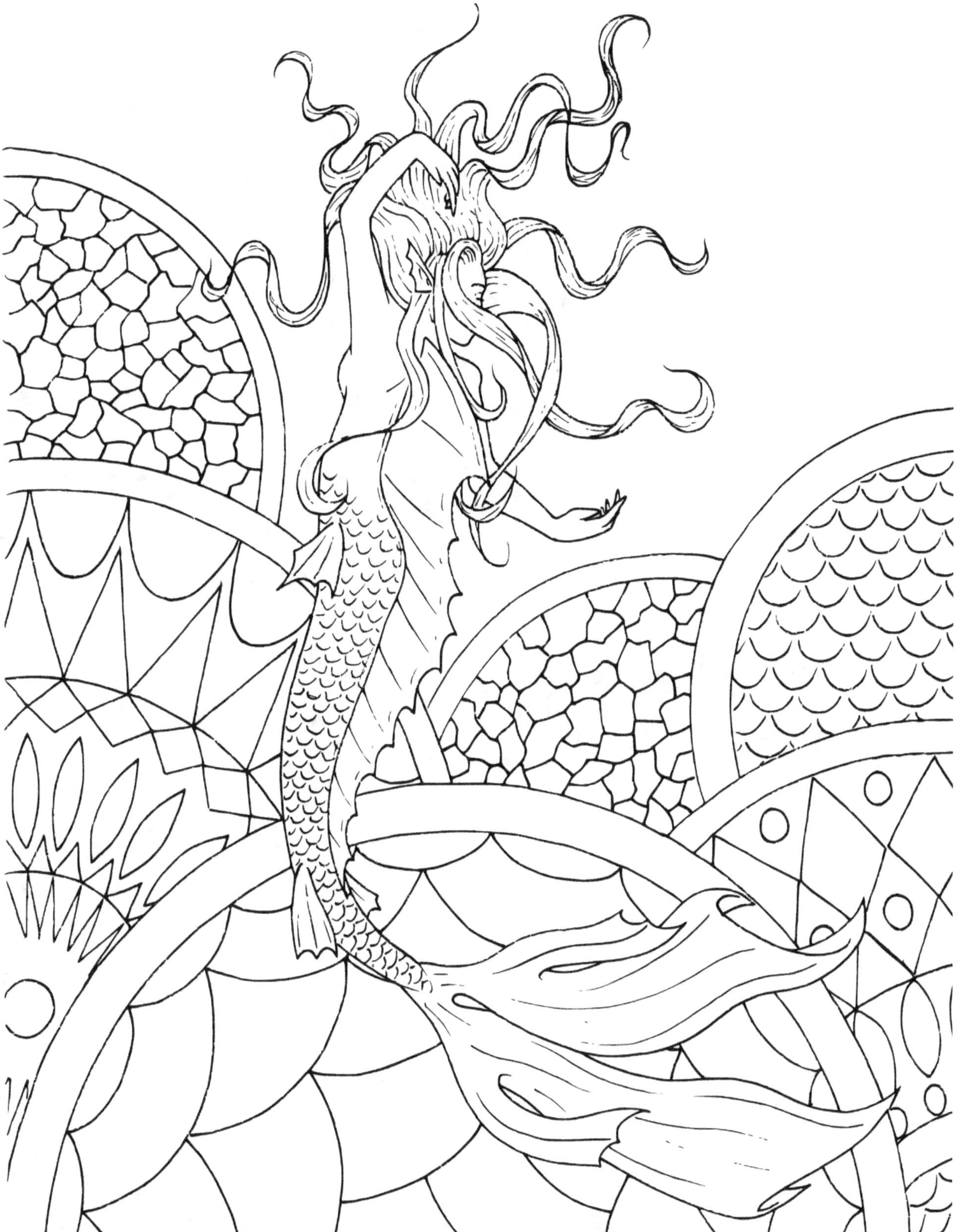

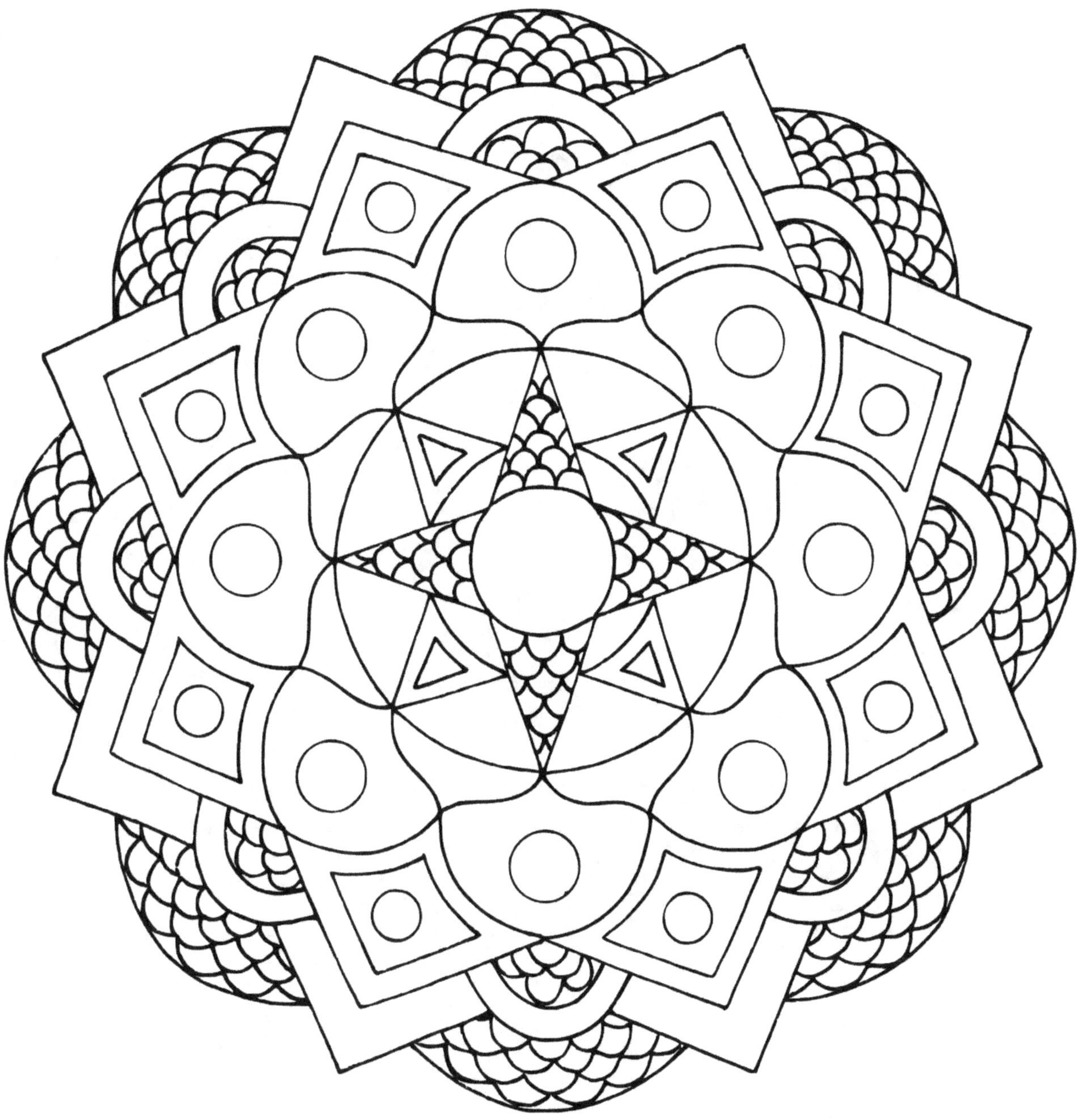

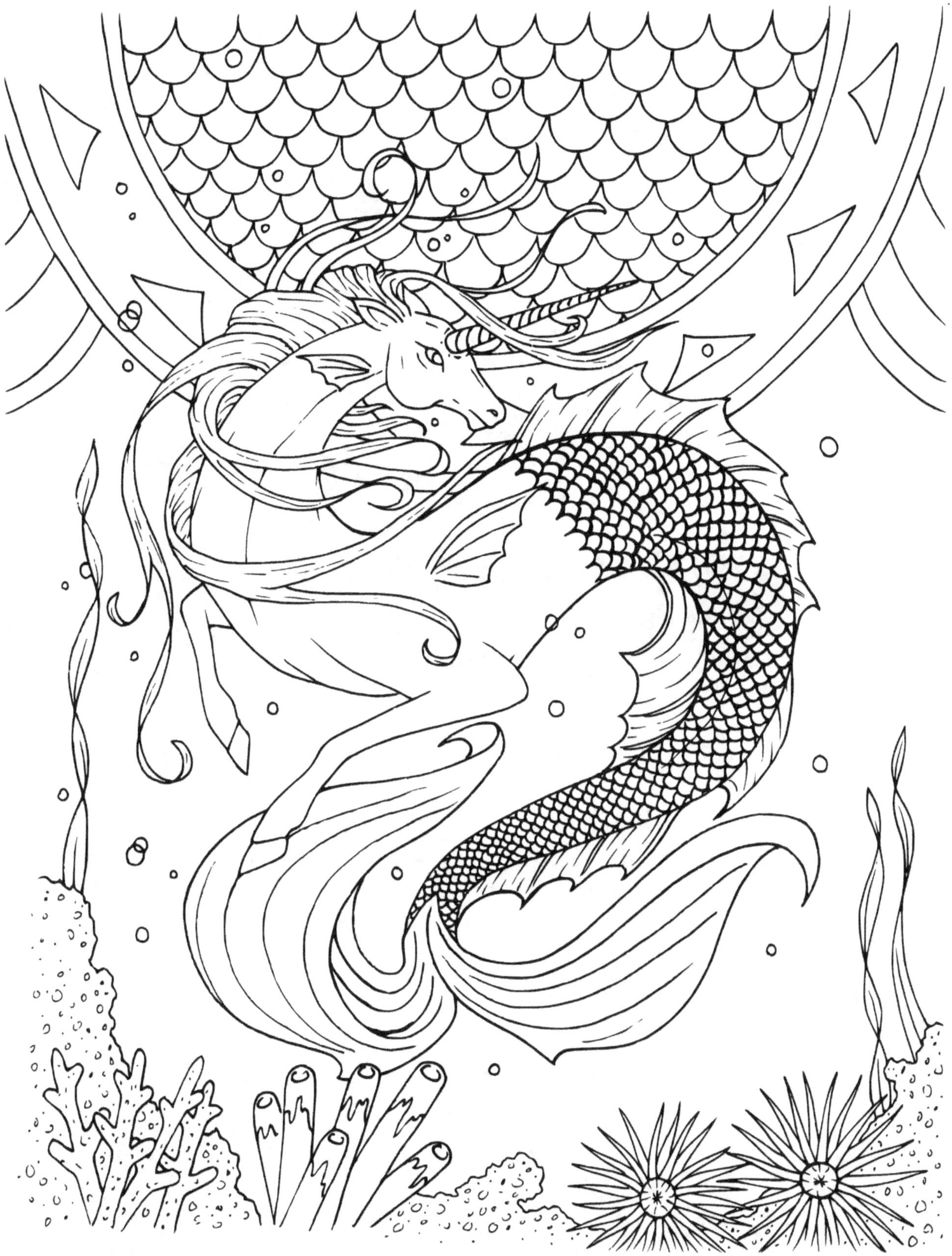

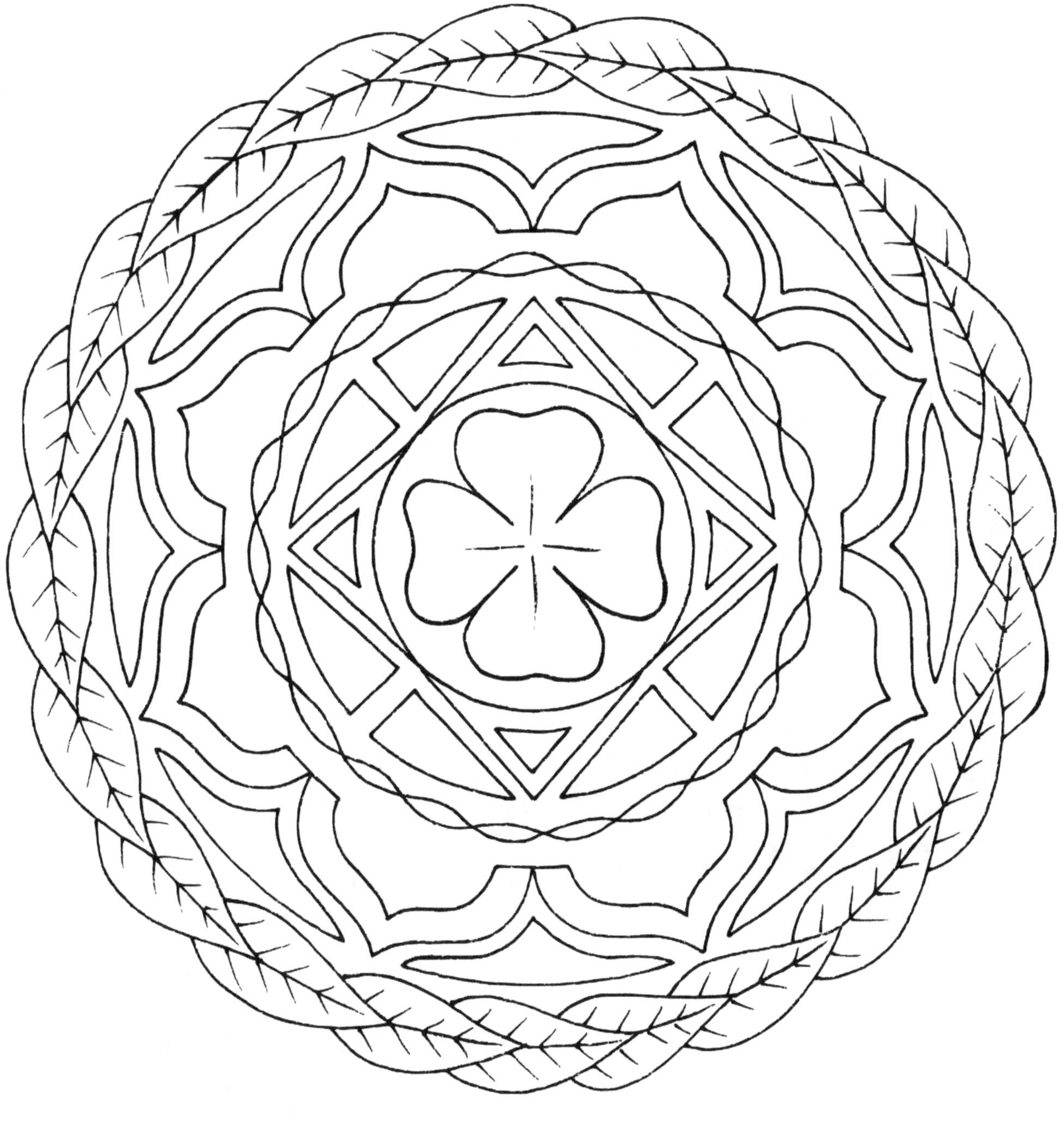

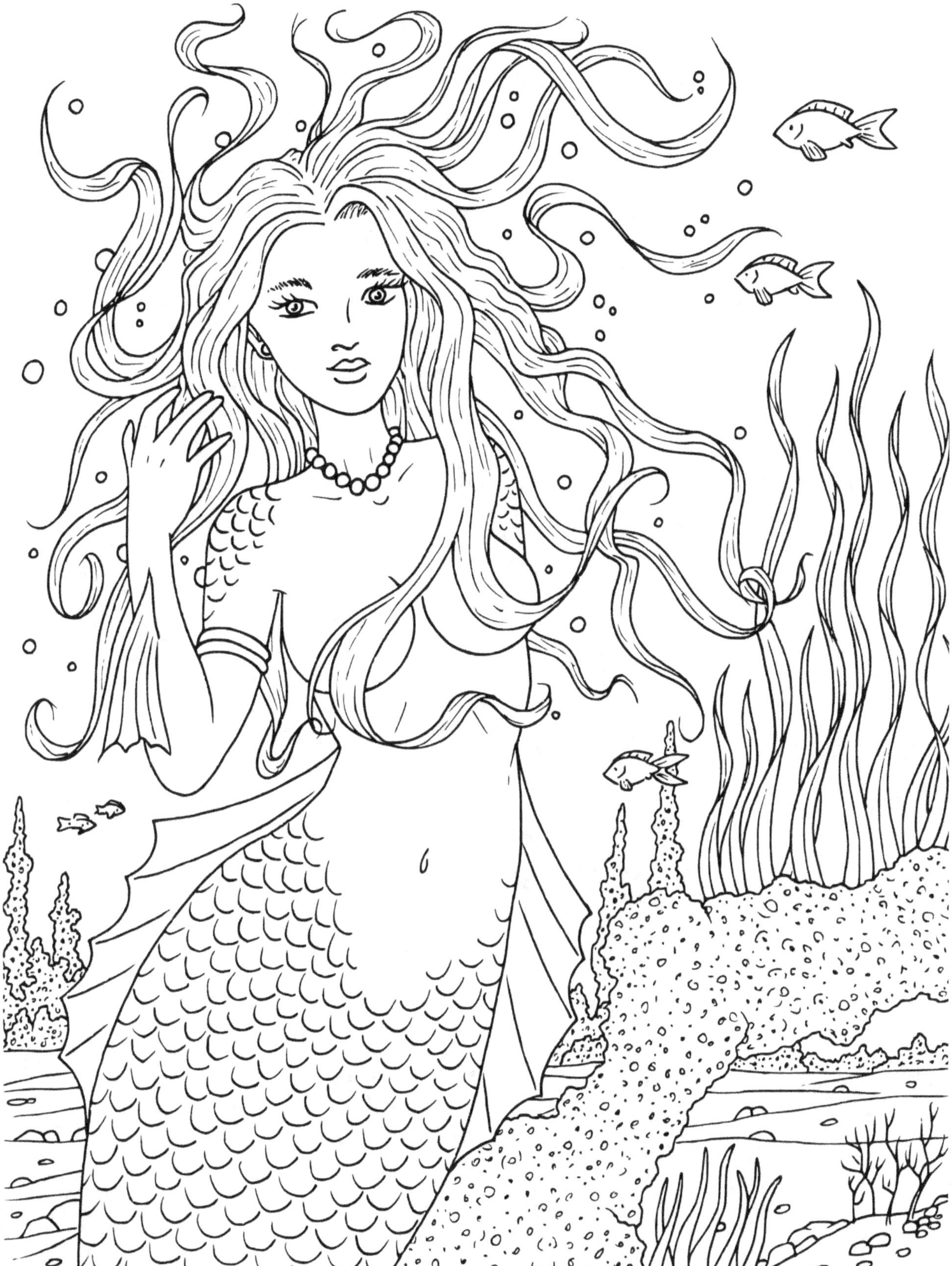

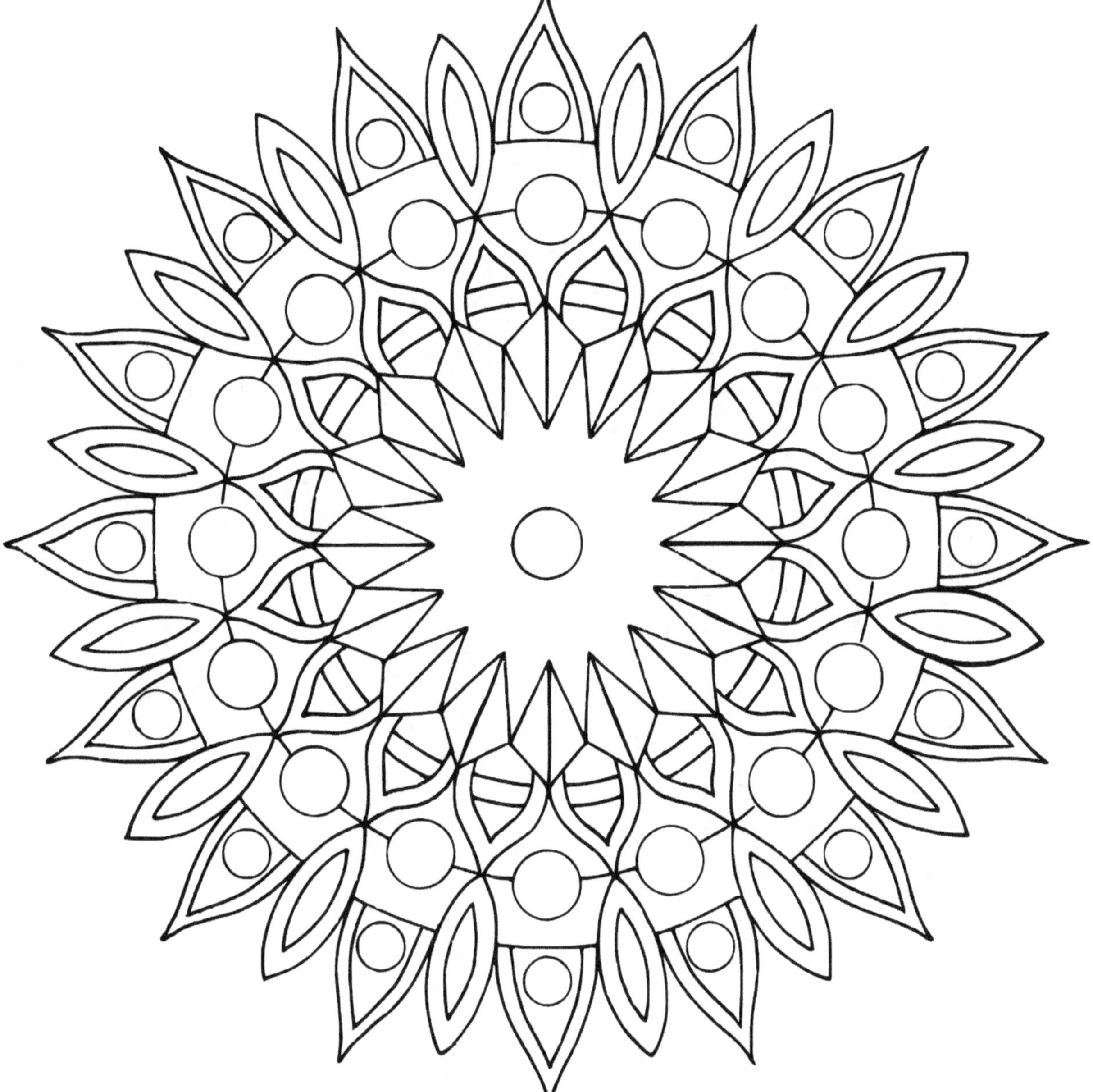

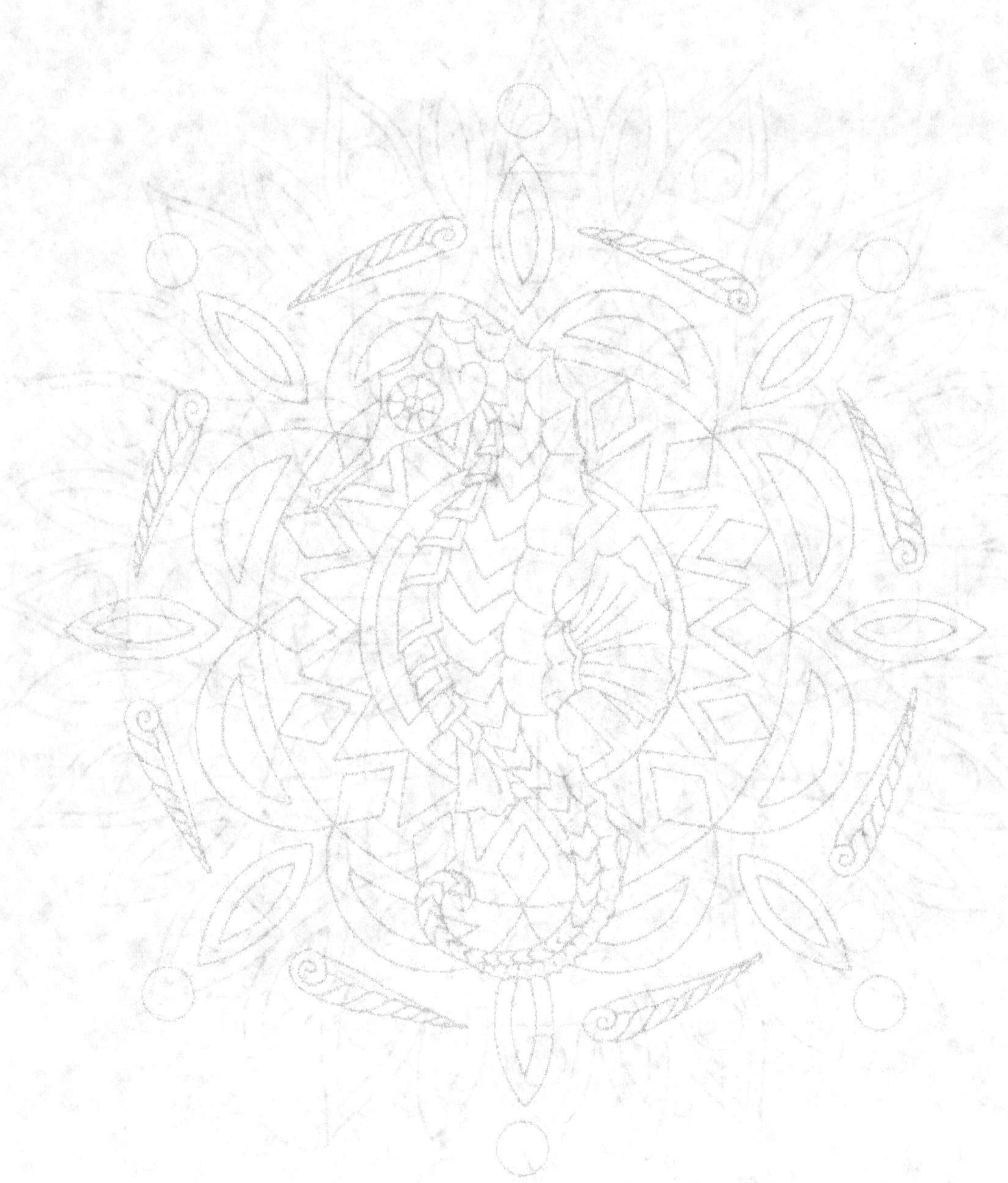

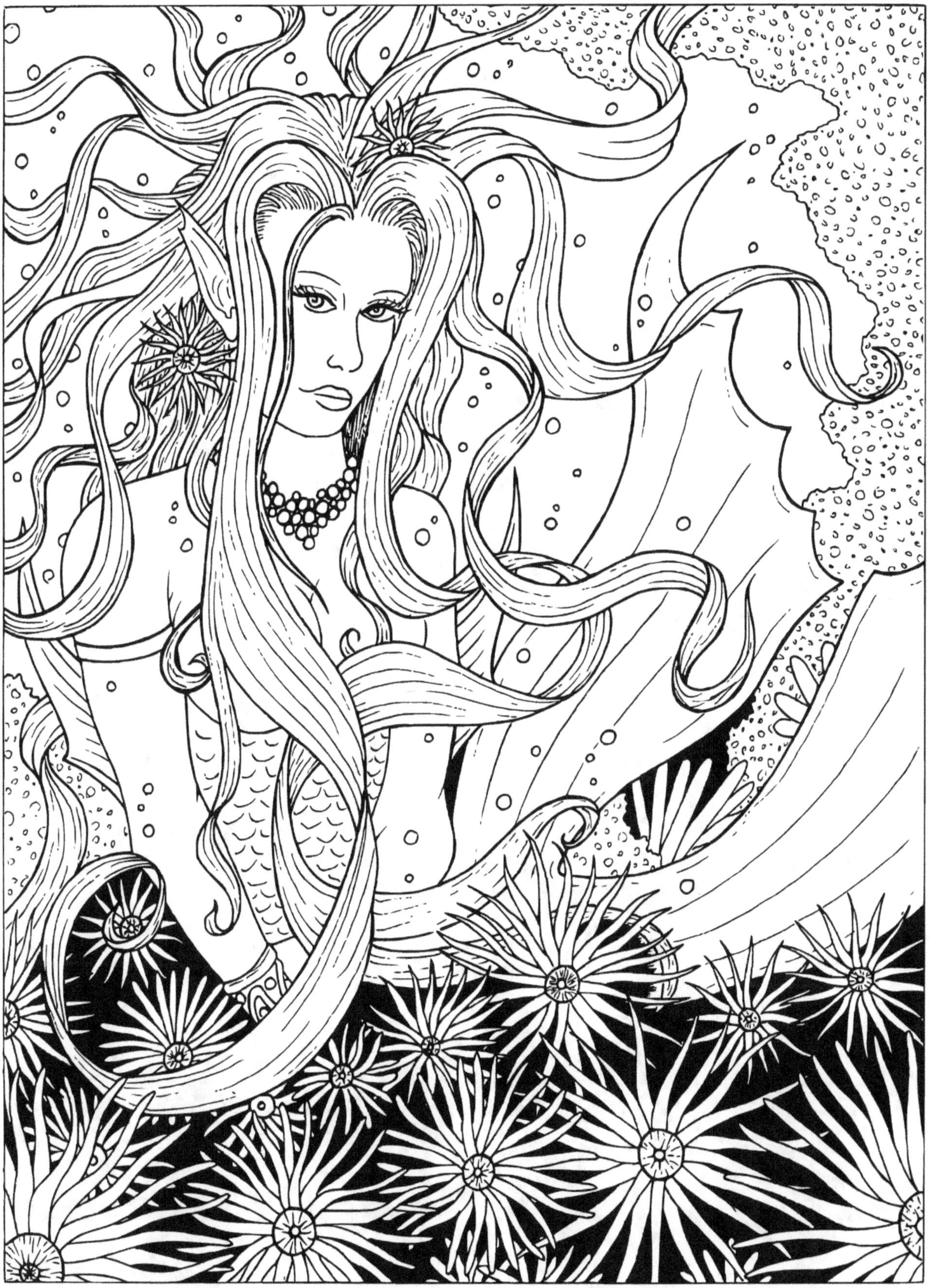

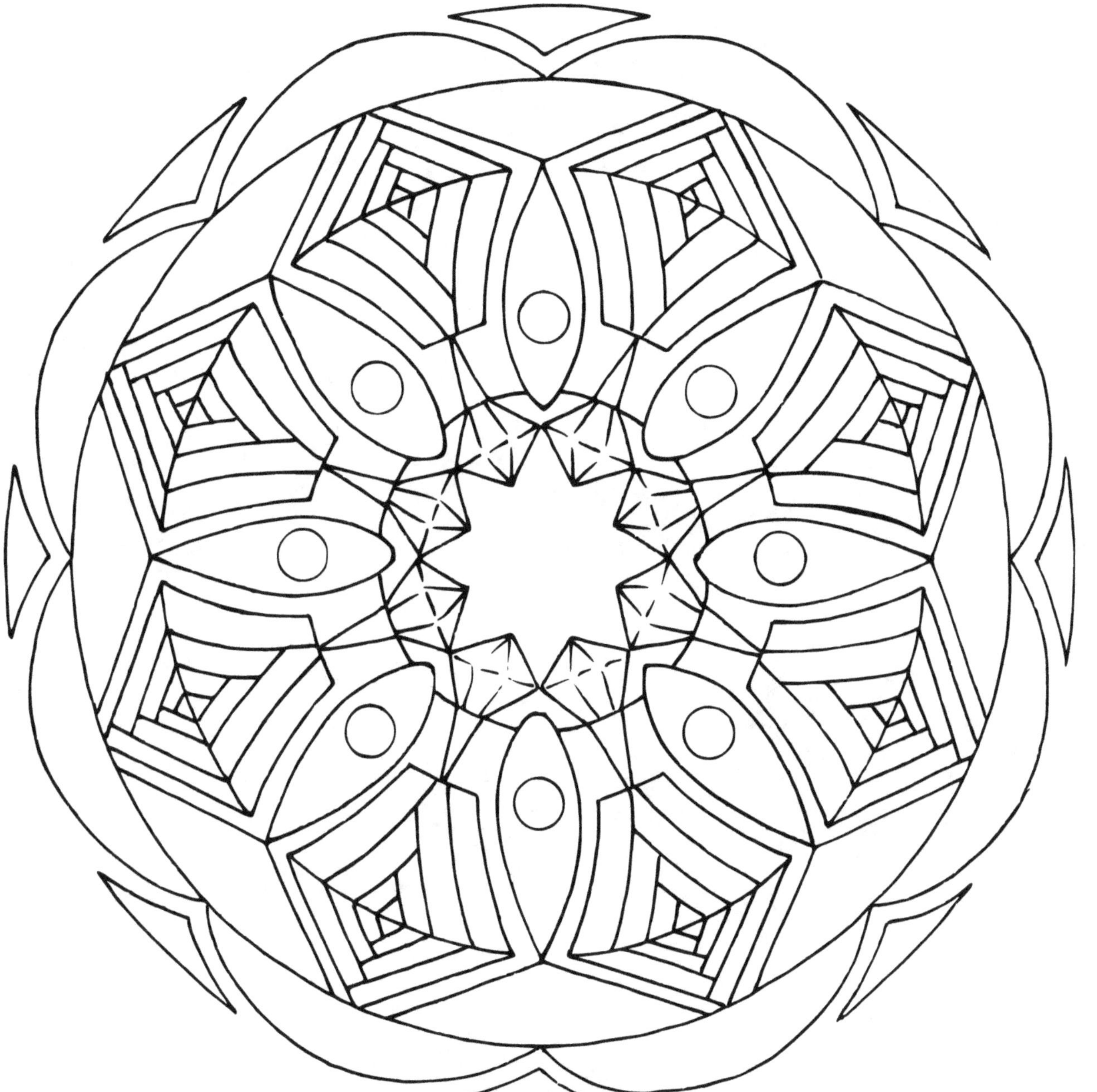

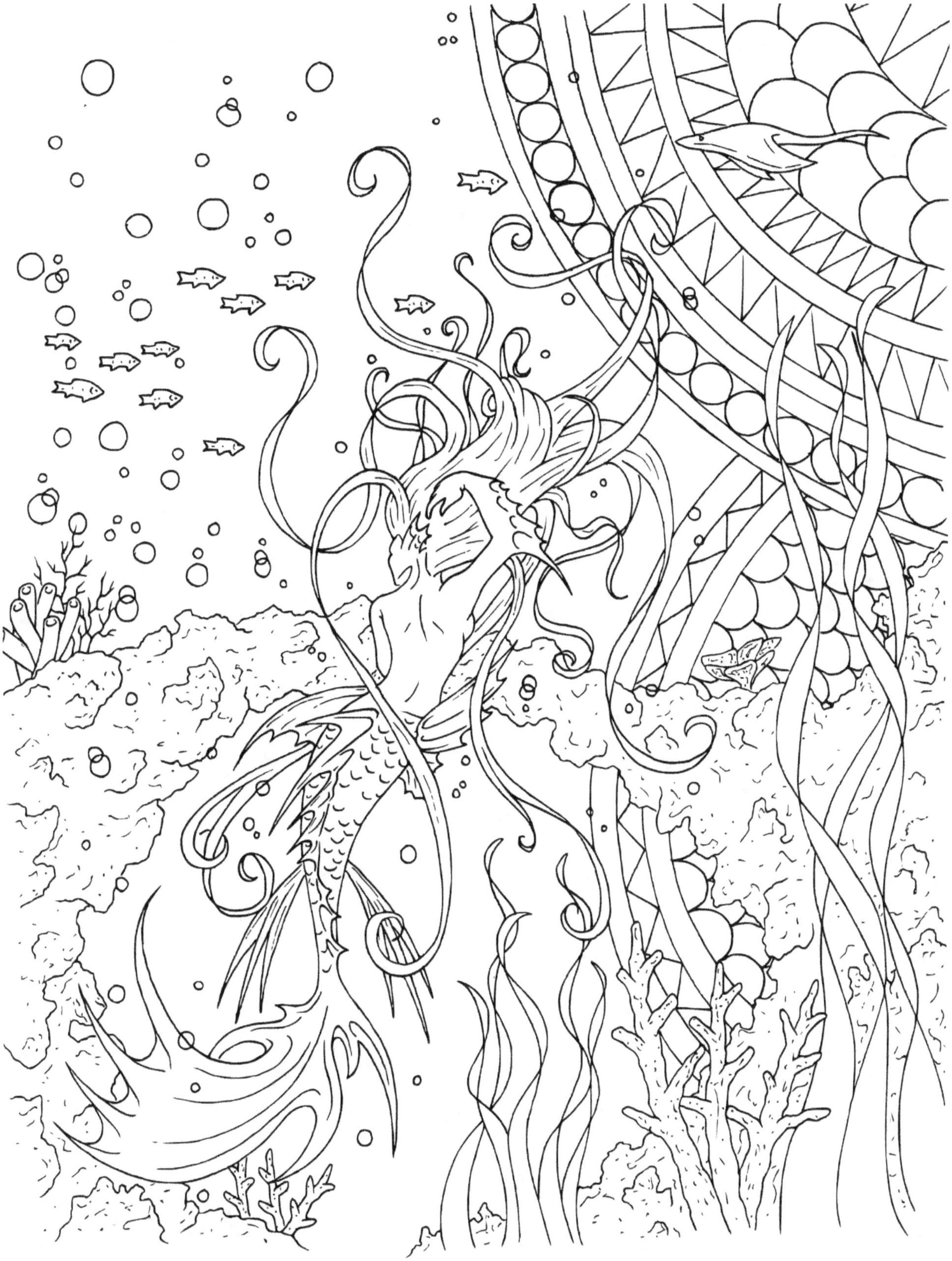

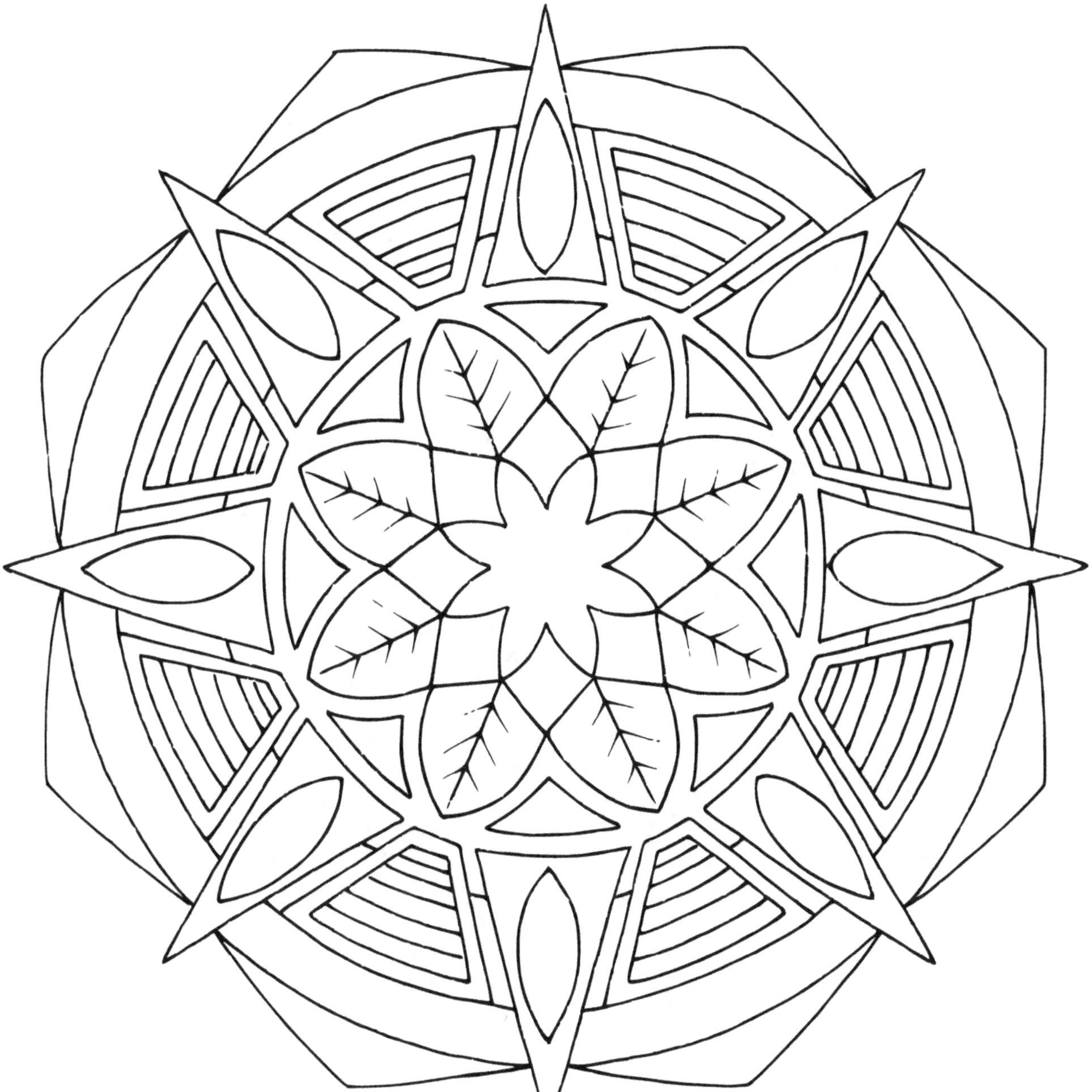

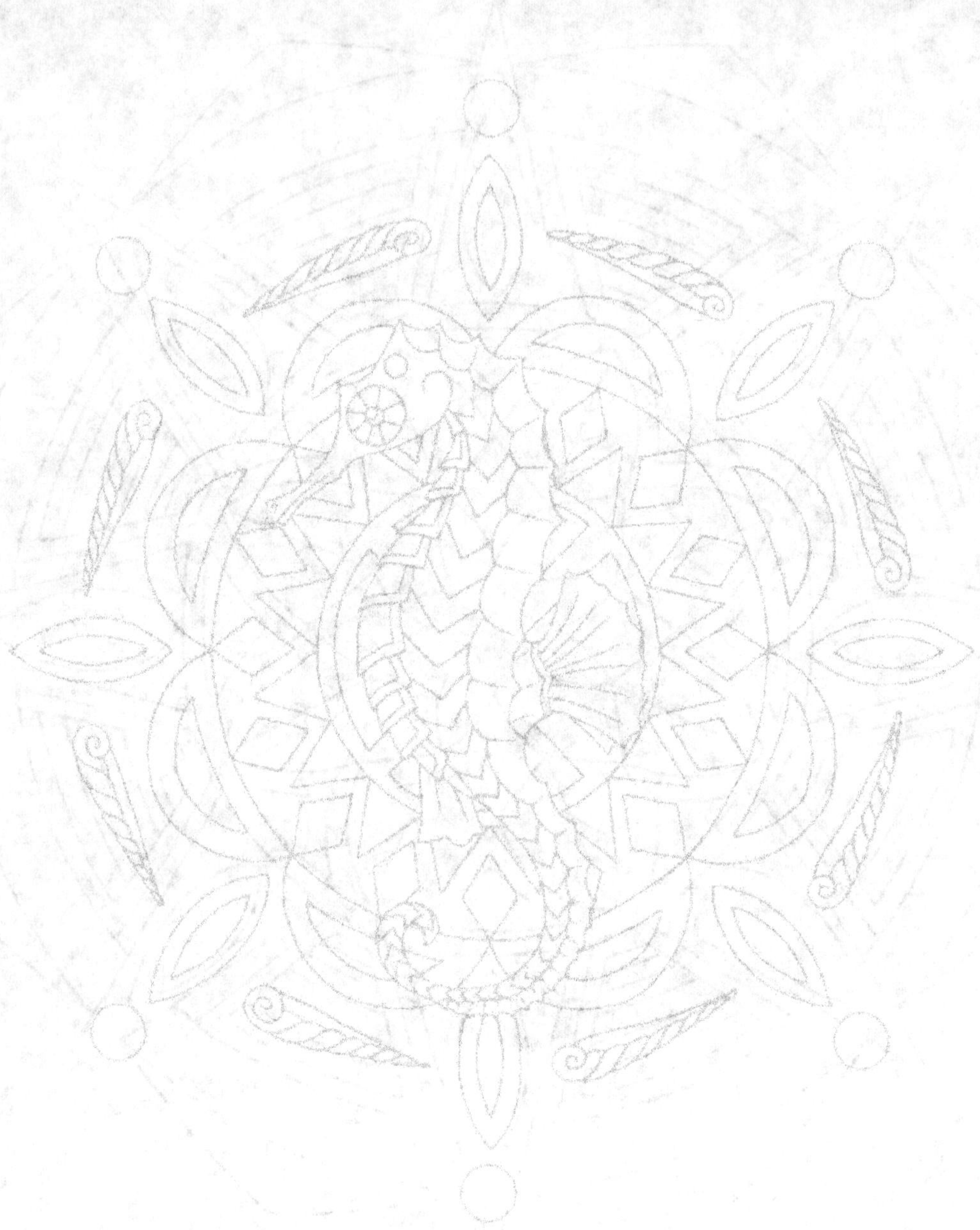

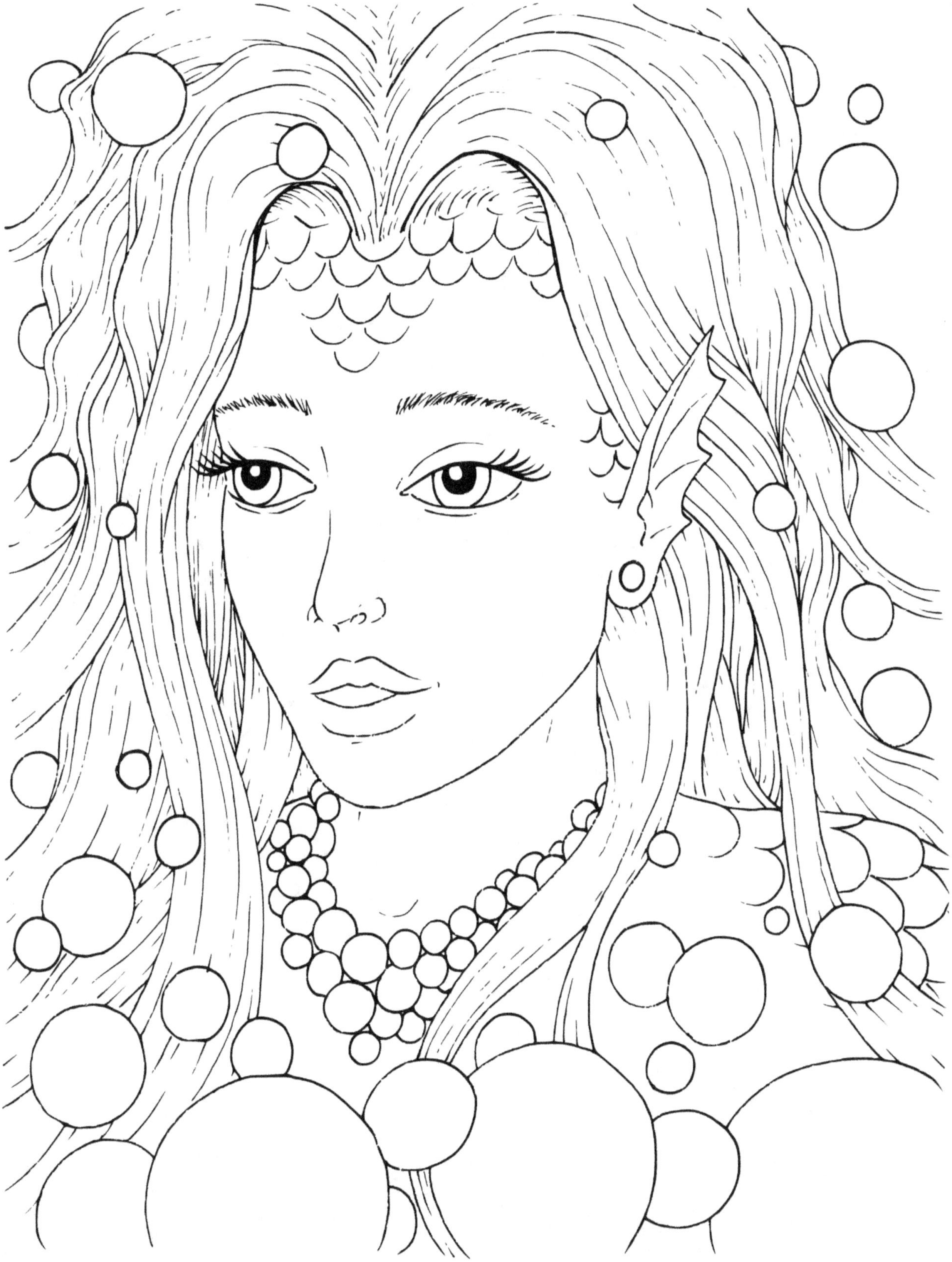

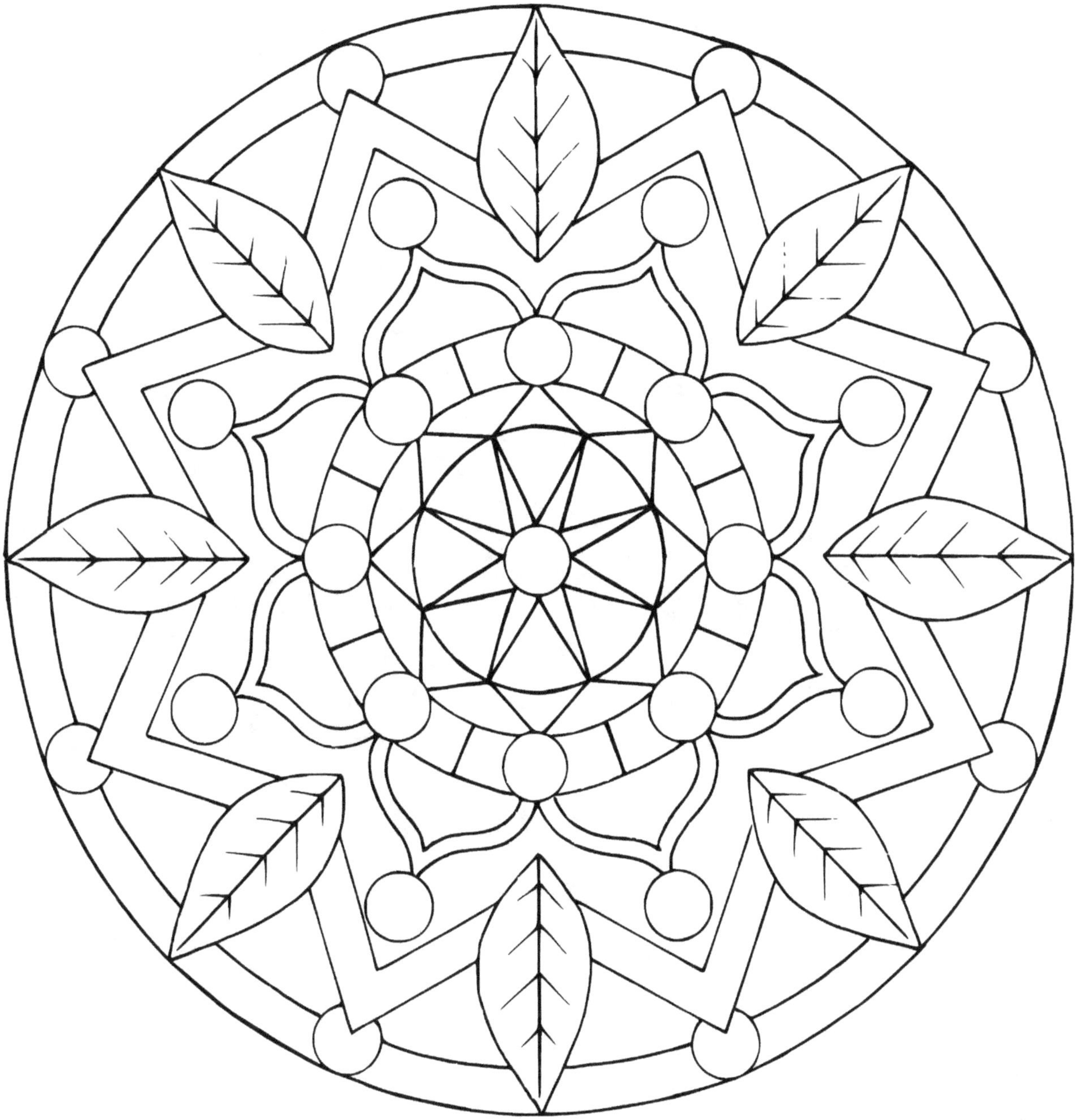

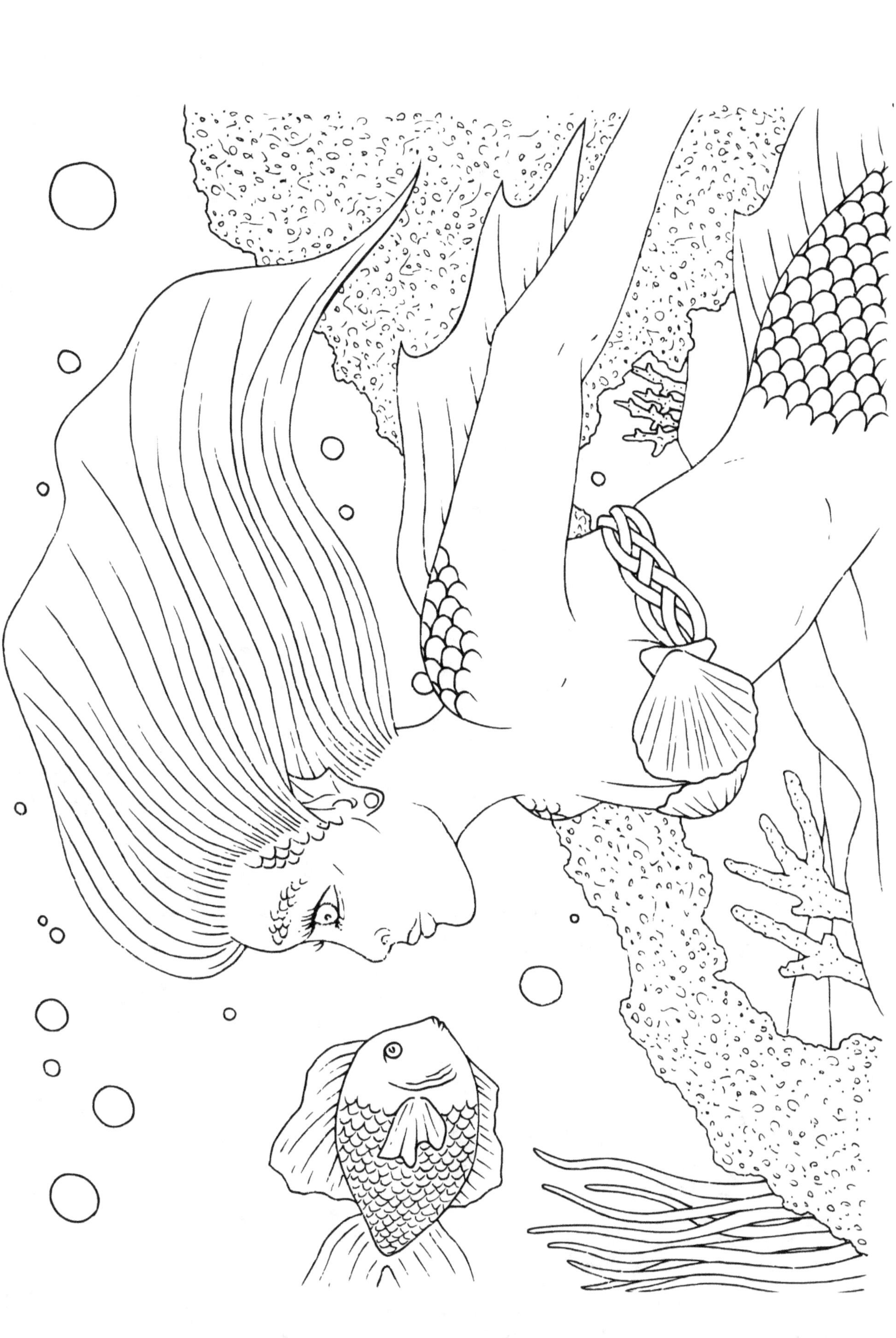

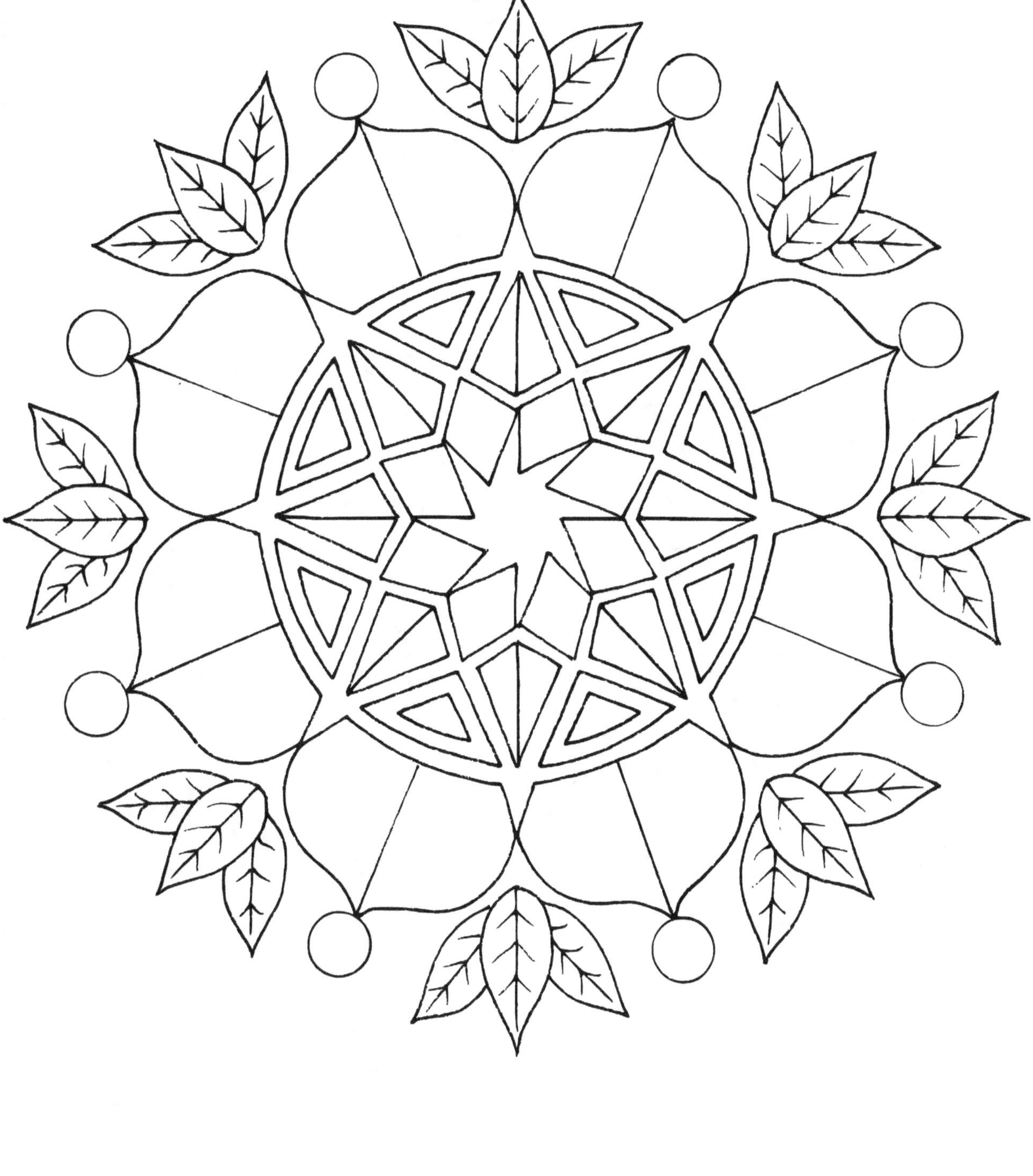

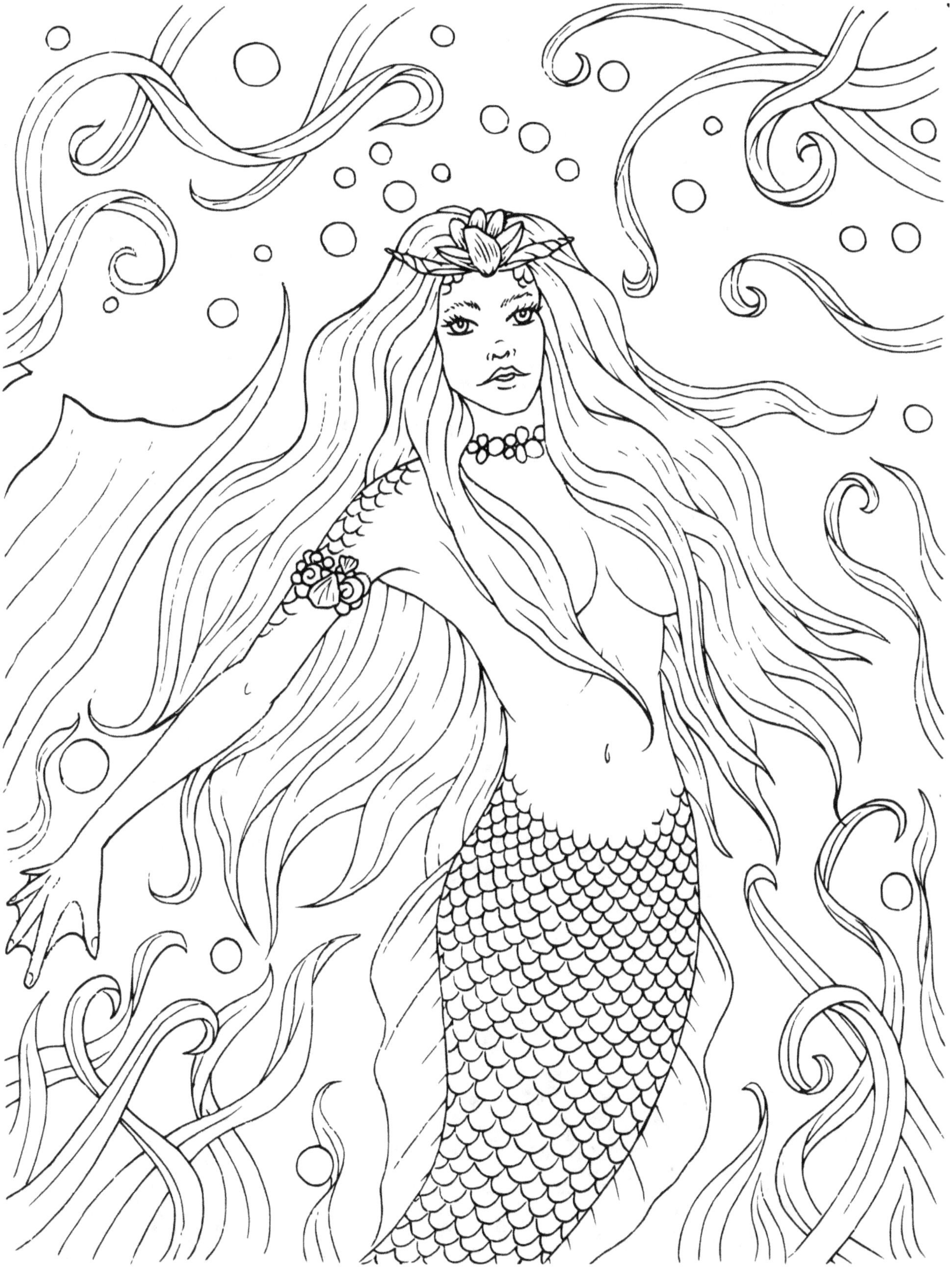

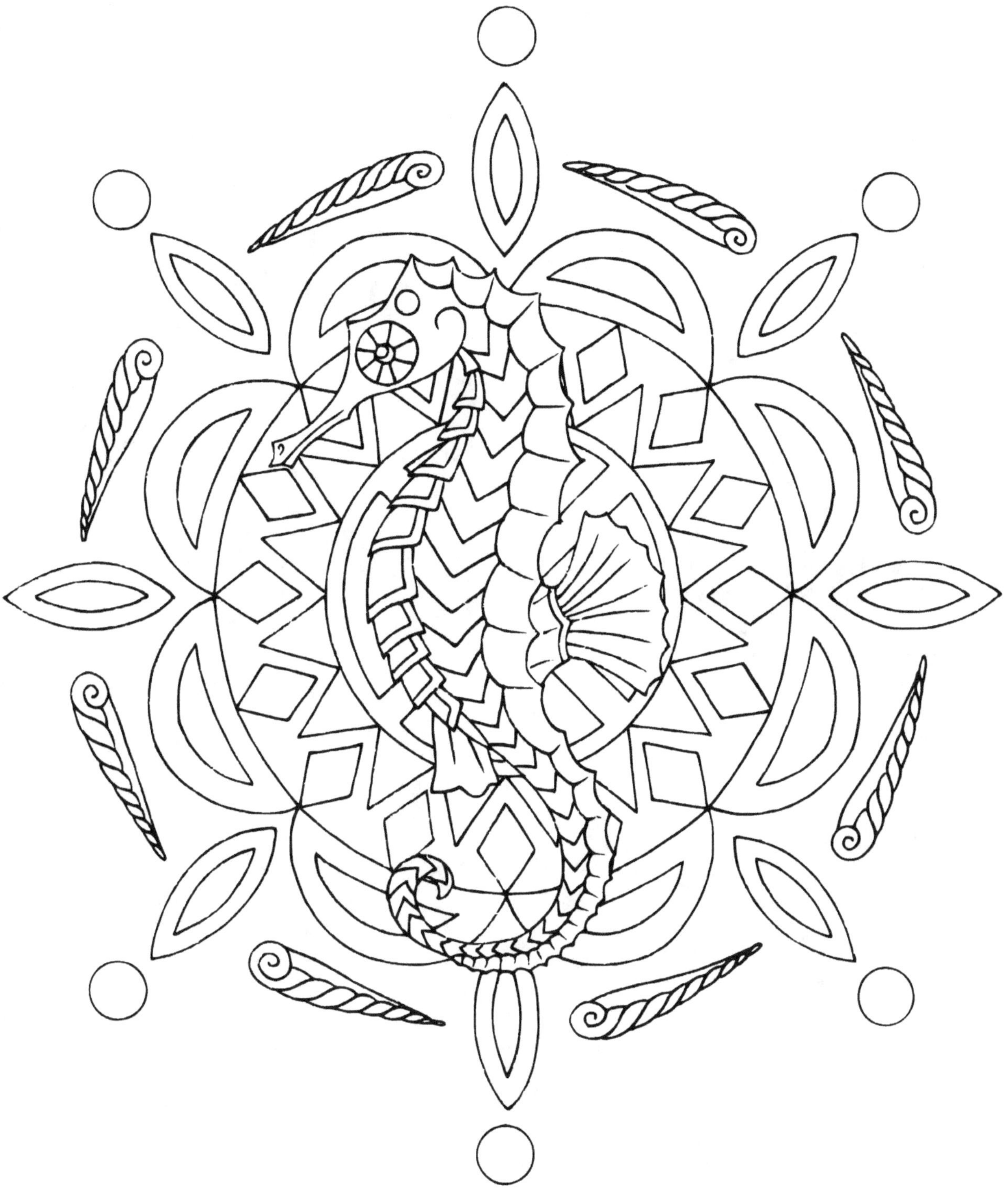

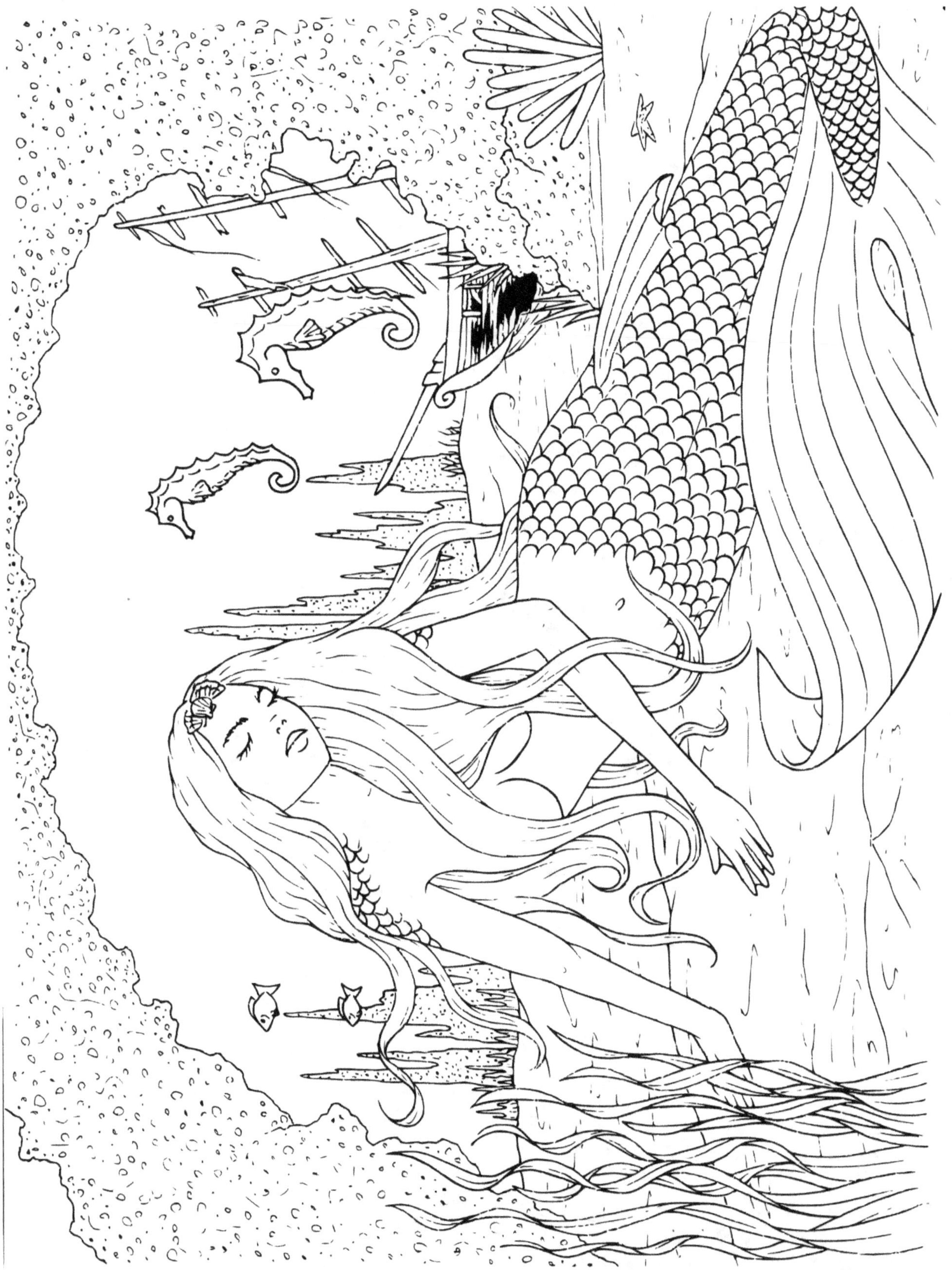

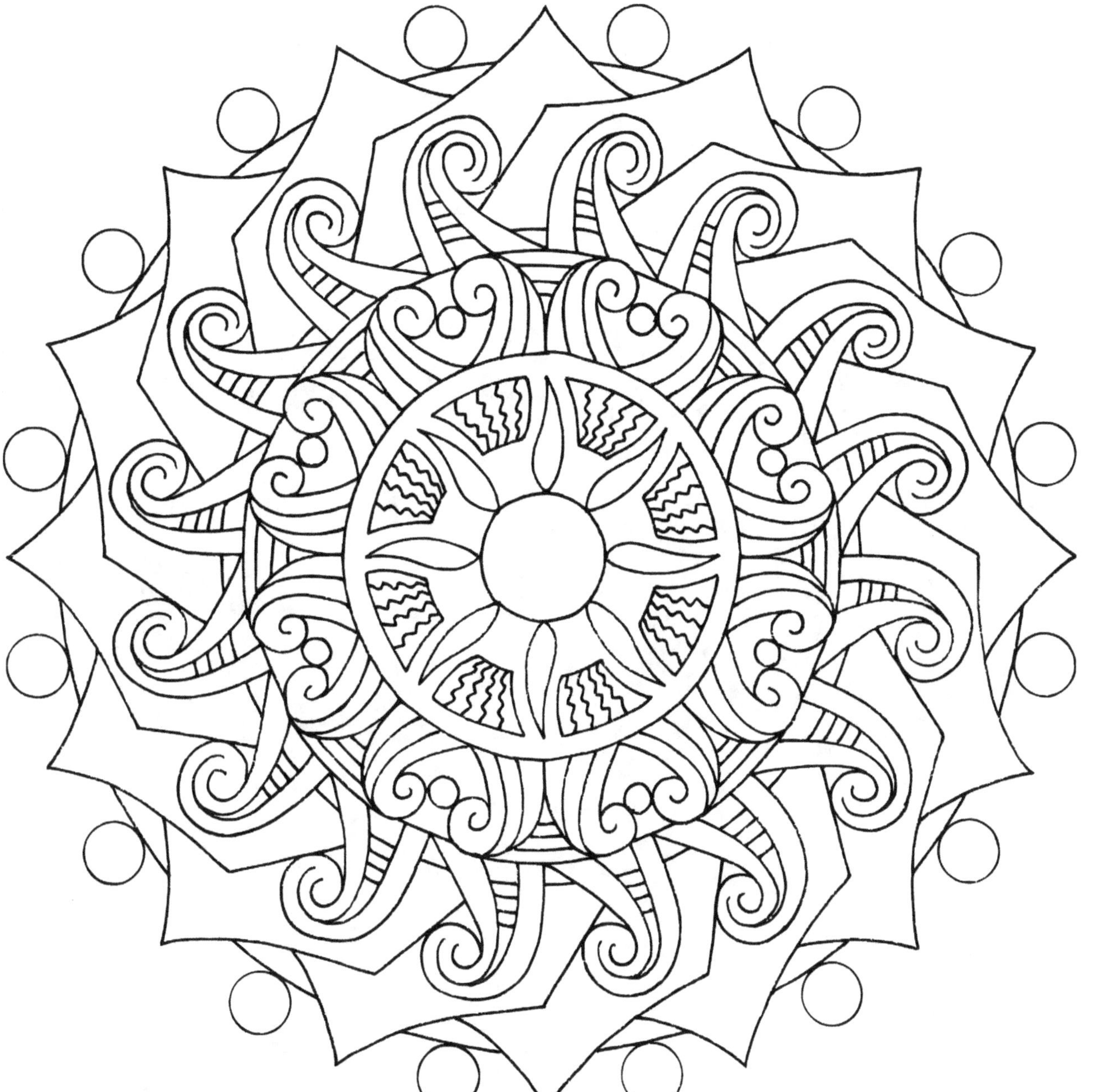

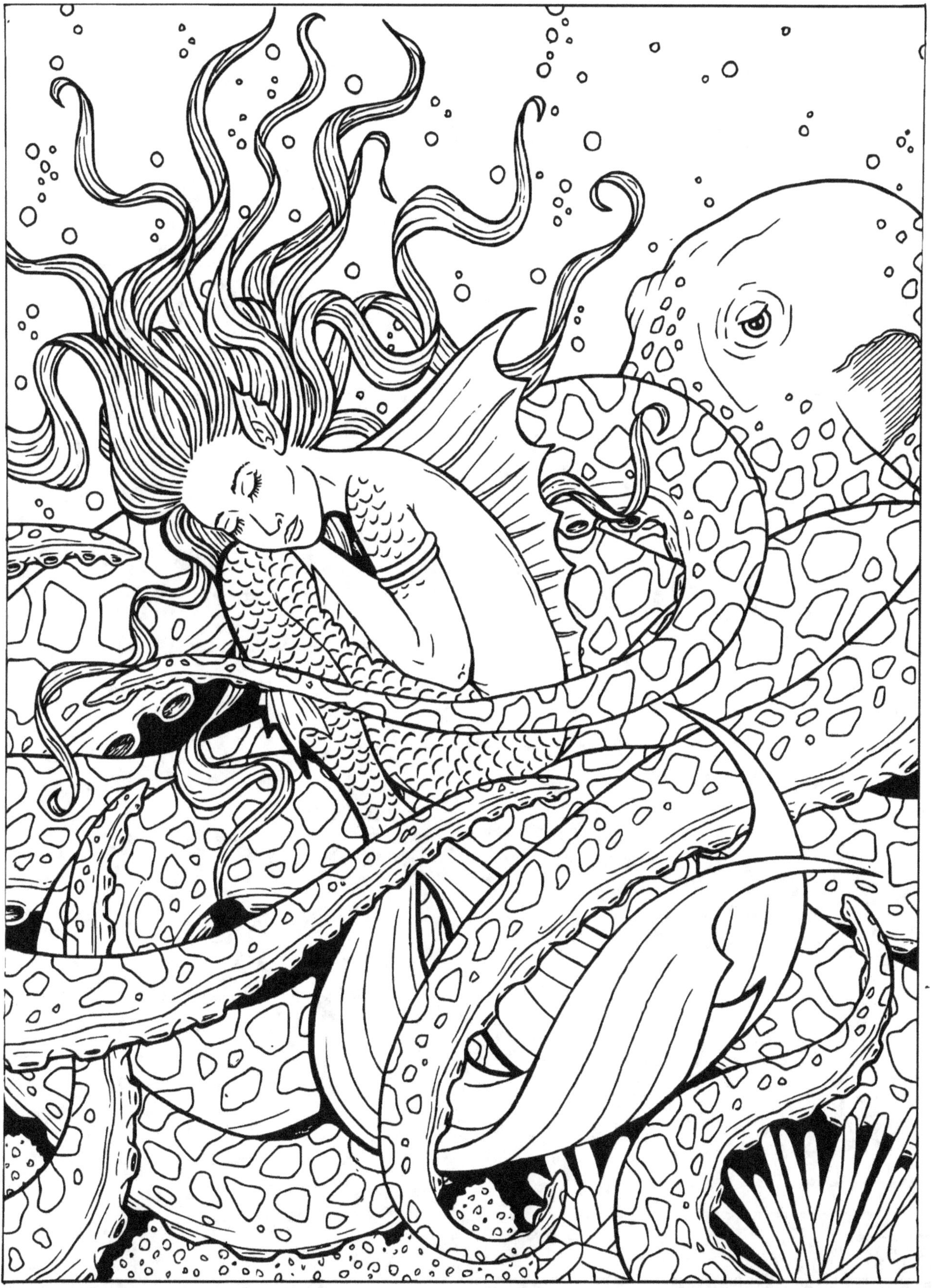

www.ingramcontent.com/pod-product-compliance
Lightning Source LLC
Chambersburg PA
CBHW081303180526
45170CB00007B/2550
9781539647461